Pardon Me, But That's a Really Stupid Sign!

Todd Hunt

Coke 49¢
2 for a dollar

**136 actual signs, ads and
product labels that will change
your life and make you rich
(OK, but they *will* make you laugh)**

Pardon Me, But That's a Really Stupid Sign!

Todd Hunt
Copyright ©MMII

Printed in the United States of America.

Third printing 2005

ISBN: 0-9723692-1-X

"Pardon Me, But That's a Really Stupid Sign!™" is a trademark of The Hunt Company and Todd Hunt, denoting a series of products that may include but is not limited to books, audio CDs and video DVDs.

Published by:
The Hunt Company
2626 N. Lakeview Avenue
Chicago, IL 60614

Ordering Information

To order more copies of this book, or to receive information about other products by Todd Hunt, please visit:

www.toddhuntspeaker.com

Also by Todd Hunt

Does Anal Retentive Have a Hyphen?

"Communication Bleeps and Blunders in Business"
Audio CD

"Todd's Take" Audio CD

"Communication Bleeps and Blunders in Business"
Video DVD

"Crafting and Marketing your Killer Keynote"
Speaker Learning System

Contents

Introduction

This book pokes fun at stupid signs, ads and product labels.

And they *should* be poked fun at, because they're just plain dumb.

Every one is real. I didn't make up any of them.

Stupid Signs

Here are some of my favorite stupid signs. They're all real I tell you. I'm not making them up.

At the back entrance of my building:

**This door
must remain
closed
at all times!**

*What good is a door if you can never open it?
Isn't that a wall??*

In the window of my local grocery store:

**Sorry,
but this is a
non-rollerblading
store**

*Why are they sorry?
I hate when I'm shopping and the store skates away.*

On a Holiday Inn marquee:

**Psychic Fair
This Saturday**

Why do they need a sign?

On the menu at Mama Luigi's Restaurant:

1/2 whole chicken

Not to be confused with a whole half-chicken.

In the window of my neighborhood dry cleaner:

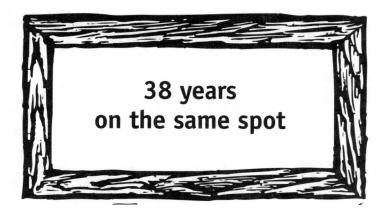

**38 years
on the same spot**

Another dry cleaner, another sign:

**Help Wanted
Bagging Girl**

She must have screwed up big time.

In the front yard of a funeral home:

**Drive carefully,
we'll wait**

In a Florida maternity ward:

No children allowed

On a maternity room door:

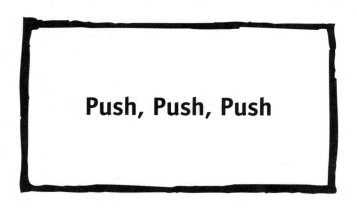

Push, Push, Push

At a tire shop in Milwaukee:

**Invite us to
your next blowout**

On the door of a plastic surgeon's office:

Hello, can we pick your nose?

In a gynecologist's office:

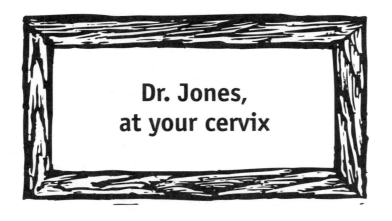

Dr. Jones,
at your cervix

In the window of Ace Hardware:

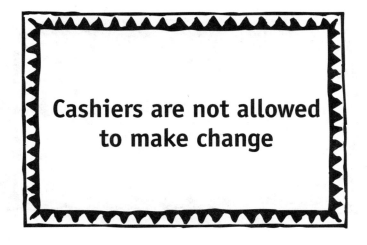

**Cashiers are not allowed
to make change**

Then what good *are they?*

In a storefront window:

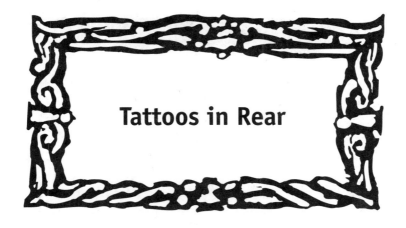

Tattoos in Rear

Now that's gotta hurt.

In another storefront window:

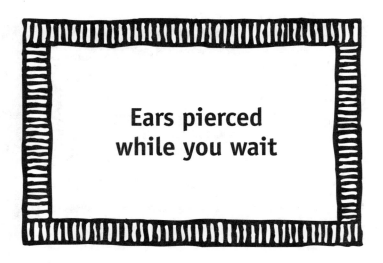

**Ears pierced
while you wait**

In a Connecticut restaurant:

**Open 7 days a week
and weekends**

On a plumber's truck:

We repair
what your
husband fixed

Outside Midas Muffler:

No appointment
necessary—
we hear you coming

In front of McDonald's:

Parking for drive-thru only

On an electrician's truck:

Let us
remove your shorts

In a Louisiana gas station:

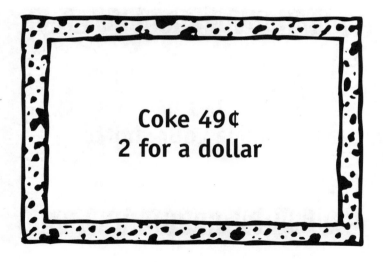

Coke 49¢
2 for a dollar

At my optometrist's office:

If you don't see
what you're looking for,
you've come to the
right place

Menu at Greco's Restaurant:

Sandwiches available daily
except after 11:00
Friday and Saturday only

OK ... when can I get a sandwich?

At a laundry shop:

How about we
refund your money,
close the store and
shoot the manager.
Would that be satisfactory?

At a towing company:

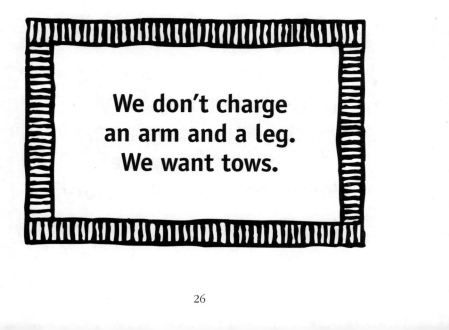

We don't charge
an arm and a leg.
We want tows.

In a taxidermist's window:

We really know our stuff

In a cemetery:

**Persons are prohibited
from picking flowers
from any but their
own graves**

In another cemetery:

No exit

On a highway:

When this sign
is under water,
road is impassable

On a building:

**Mental Health
Prevention Center**

On an automatic hand dryer:

**Do not activate
with wet hands**

In a shoe repair shop:

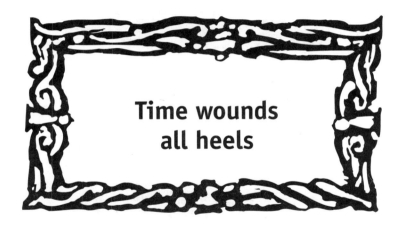

Time wounds
all heels

In an Ohio restaurant:

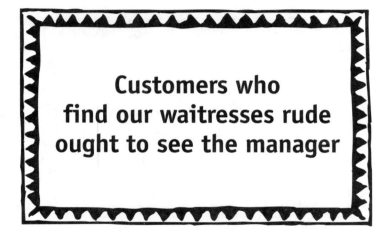

**Customers who
find our waitresses rude
ought to see the manager**

In a Tampa restaurant:

Kooks Wanted
Experience Required

In a Sioux Falls restaurant:

**Don't stand there
and be hungry.
Come on in
and get fed up.**

On the grounds of a private school:

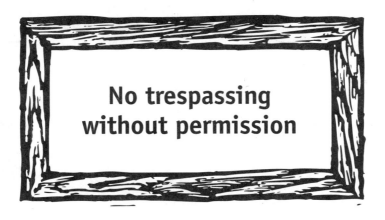

No trespassing
without permission

On a Lutheran church door:

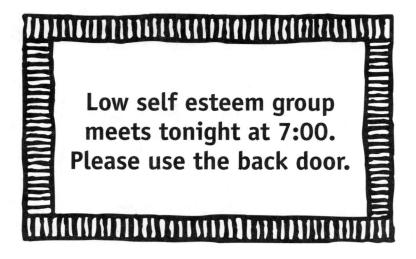

Low self esteem group
meets tonight at 7:00.
Please use the back door.

In another Lutheran church parking lot:

**Parking for parishioners only.
Violators will be confirmed.**

On a booster seat at Kentucky Fried Chicken
(sorry, I mean KFC):

**Do not remove
or cover this label**

So where do we put the darn kid?

In a Los Angeles dance hall:

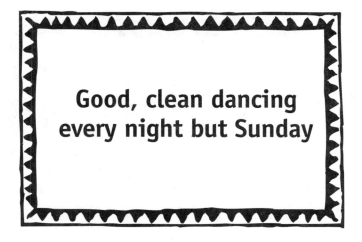

**Good, clean dancing
every night but Sunday**

In a Pittsburgh drugstore:

We dispense with accuracy

In the office of a loan company:

Ask about our plans
for owning your home

In a veterinarian's waiting room:

**Be back in five minutes.
Sit! Stay!**

At a propane filling station:

**Tank heaven
for little grills**

On a convalescent home:

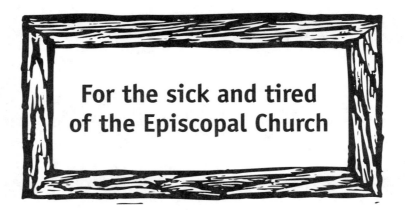

For the sick and tired
of the Episcopal Church

In a Maine shop window:

Our motto is to
give our customers
the lowest possible prices
and workmanship.

At a clinic:

Planned Parenthood
Enter in the Rear

In a funeral home:

Ask about our
layaway plan

In a clothing store:

Wonderful bargains for men with 16 and 17 necks

At a radiator repair garage:

Best place to take a leak

In a public shower in Colorado:

**Please pay
before showering
at front desk**

In the vestry of a New England Church:

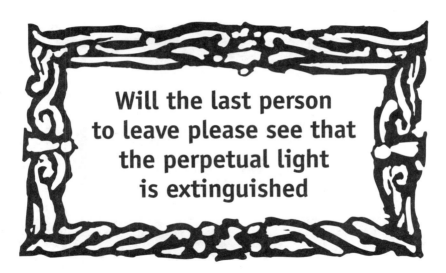

Will the last person
to leave please see that
the perpetual light
is extinguished

On an Oregon hotel message board:

**Laubach Litracy
National Conference**

In a Virginia family-owned grocery store:

**You can't
beat our meat**

On the wall of a Baltimore estate:

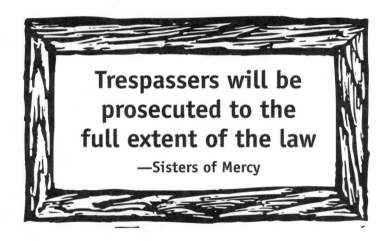

Trespassers will be prosecuted to the full extent of the law

—Sisters of Mercy

In the men's room in a Chicago restaurant:

Please do not dispose of anything in the toilet

Stupid Signs in Foreign Countries

Hey, English is not their first language, so go easy. But these signs are still funny.

In a Chinese pet store:

**Buy one dog,
get one flea**

In a Tokyo hotel:

**It is forbidden to
steal hotel towels please.
If you are not person
to do such thing is please
not to read notice.**

In a Bucharest hotel lobby:

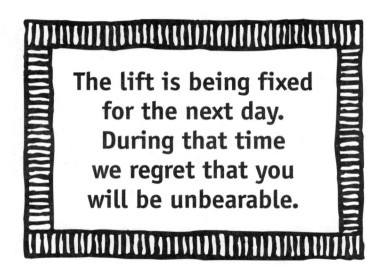

The lift is being fixed
for the next day.
During that time
we regret that you
will be unbearable.

In a Leipzig elevator:

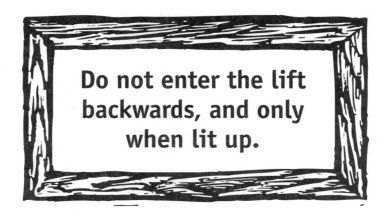

Do not enter the lift
backwards, and only
when lit up.

In a Belgrade hotel elevator:

**To move the cabin, push
button for wishing floor.
If the cabin should enter more
persons, each one should
press a number of wishing floor.
Driving is then going
alphabetically by national order.**

In a hotel in Athens:

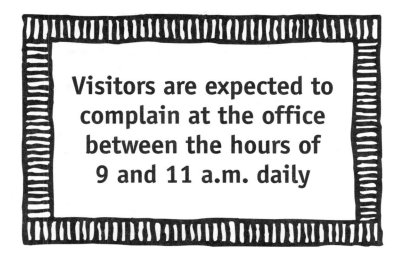

Visitors are expected to complain at the office between the hours of 9 and 11 a.m. daily

In a Yugoslavian hotel:

The flattening of underwear with pleasure is the job of the chambermaid

From a brochure of a car rental firm in Tokyo:

When passenger of foot
heave in sight, tootle
the horn. Trumpet him
melodiously at first,
but if he still obstacles
your passage then
tootle him with vigor.

In the lobby of a Moscow hotel across from a Russian Orthodox monastery:

You are welcome to visit the cemetery where famous Russian and Soviet composers, artists and writers are buried daily except Thursday

In an Austrian hotel catering to skiers:

Not to perambulate the corridors in the hours of repose in the boots of ascension

On the menu in a Swiss restaurant:

Our wines leave you
nothing to hope for

Outside a Hong Kong tailor shop:

Ladies may have
a fit upstairs

Outside a Paris Dress shop:

**Dresses for
street walking**

In Germany's Black Forest:

It is strictly forbidden on
our black forest camping site
that people of different sex,
for instance, men and women,
live together in one tent
unless they are married with
each other for that purpose

From a Japanese information booklet
about using hotel air conditioner:

**Cooles and heates:
if you want just
condition of warm
in your room,
please control yourself.**

In a Zurich hotel:

> **Because of the impropriety of entertaining guests of the opposite sex in the bedroom it is suggested that the lobby be used for this purpose**

In an ad by a Hong Kong dentist:

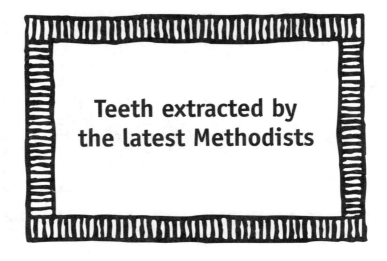

Teeth extracted by
the latest Methodists

In a Rome laundry:

Ladies, leave your
clothes here and spend
the afternoon having
a good time

In a Czechoslovakian tourist agency:

Take one of our
horse-driven city tours.
We guarantee
no miscarriages.

In a Japanese hotel:

You are invited to
take advantage of
the chambermaid

In a Swiss mountain inn:

**Special today:
no ice cream**

In a Copenhagen airline ticket office:

**We take your bags
and send them in
all directions**

On the door of a Moscow hotel room:

If this is your
first visit to the USSR,
you are welcome to it

In a Norwegian cocktail lounge:

**Ladies are requested
not to have children
in the bar**

On the menu of a Polish hotel:

Salad a firm's own make;
limpid red beet soup with
cheesy dumplings in the form
of a finger; roasted duck
let loose; beef rashers beaten up
in the country people's fashion.

At a Budapest zoo:

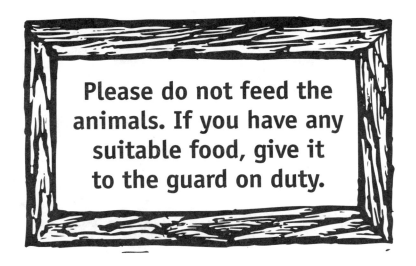

Please do not feed the animals. If you have any suitable food, give it to the guard on duty.

In the office of a Roman doctor:

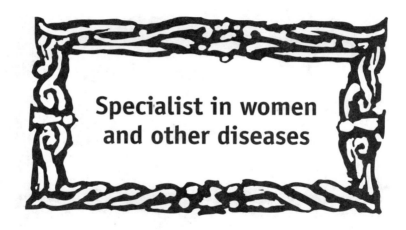

Specialist in women
and other diseases

In an Acapulco hotel:

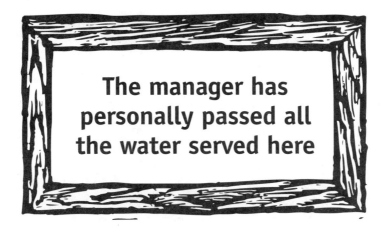

The manager has personally passed all the water served here

In a Tokyo shop:

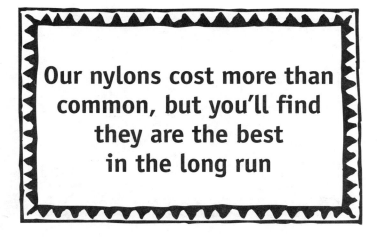

Our nylons cost more than
common, but you'll find
they are the best
in the long run

In a Rhodes tailor shop:

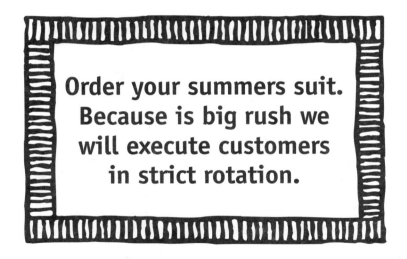

Order your summers suit.
Because is big rush we
will execute customers
in strict rotation.

Two signs from a Majorca shop entrance:

English well talking

Here speeching American

In a Bangkok temple:

It is forbidden to enter
a woman even a
foreigner if dressed
as a man

In a Thailand hotel lobby:

Please do not bring solicitors into your room

In brochure for an Italian hotel:

> **This hotel is renowned for its peace and solitude. In fact, crowds from all over the world flock here to enjoy its solitude.**

In a Hong Kong supermarket:

For your convenience,
we recommend
courteous, efficient
self-service

In a Paris hotel elevator:

**Please leave
your values at the
front desk**

In a Bangkok dry cleaner:

Drop your trousers here for the best results

In a Tokyo bar:

**Special cocktails
for the ladies
with nuts**

In an East African newspaper:

A new swimming pool is rapidly taking shape since the contractors have thrown in the bulk of their workers

In a Vienna hotel:

In case of fire,
do your utmost to
alarm the hotel porter

Ad for donkey rides in Thailand:

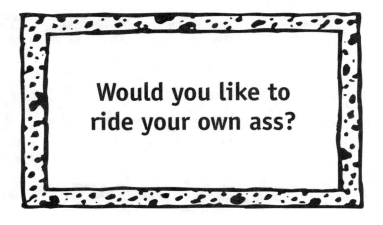

Would you like to
ride your own ass?

Hotel menu at Italian inn:

Any day or night
our chef will throw up
his favorite pasta dish
for you

Menu items at a Bucharest restaurant:

**Chicken soup
with droppings**

**Chicken roasted
in spit**

In a Tokyo hotel's rules and regulations:

**Guests are requested
not to smoke or
do other disgusting
behaviors in bed**

Sign in a German hotel room:

If you wish for breakfast
in your bedroom, just lift
your telephone and speak
to the receptionist.
This will be enough to
bring your food up.

From the Soviet Weekly:

There will be a Moscow Exhibition of Arts by 15,000 Soviet Republic painters and sculptors. These were executed over the past two years.

Stupid Product Labels

Manufacturers must think consumers are idiots. Unfortunately, many of them *are*.

So here are some actual product labels to make you laugh.

Be thankful *you're* not stupid.

On packaging for a Rowenta iron:

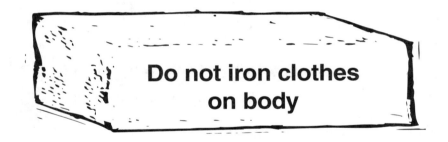

Do not iron clothes on body

On a bar of Dial soap:

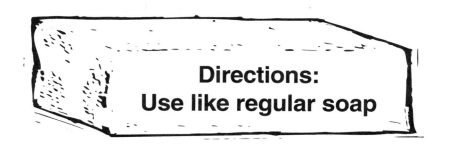

Directions:
Use like regular soap

On Boot's Children's cough medicine:

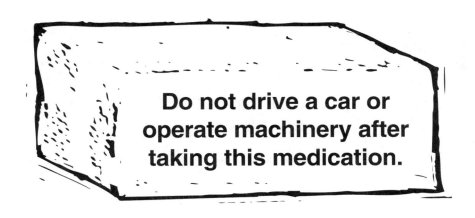

Do not drive a car or operate machinery after taking this medication.

On Sainsbury's peanuts:

On an American Airlines package of peanuts:

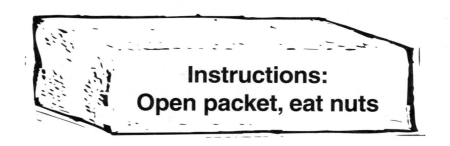

**Instructions:
Open packet, eat nuts**

On a Sears hairdryer:

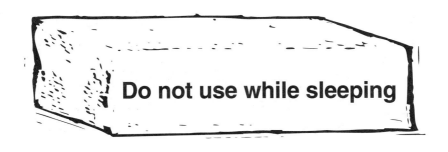

Gee, that's the only time I have to work on my hair!

On Tesco's Tiramisu dessert
(printed on bottom):

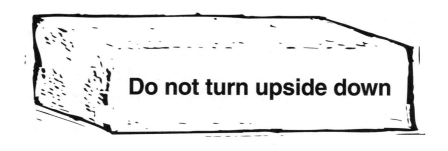

Too late!

On a child's Superman costume:

Wearing of this garment does not enable you to fly

On box of Nytol sleeping pills:

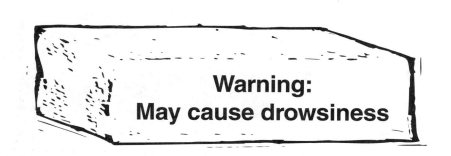

**Warning:
May cause drowsiness**

On a bag of Fritos:

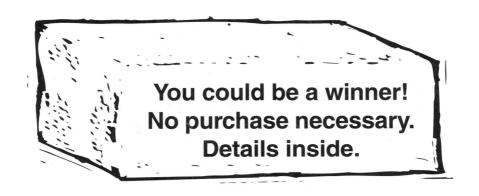

**You could be a winner!
No purchase necessary.
Details inside.**

The shoplifter special

On Marks & Spencer bread pudding:

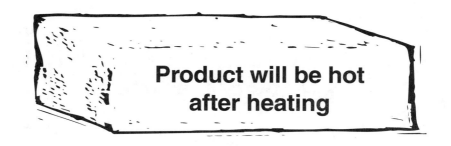

Product will be hot after heating

On a Swanson frozen dinner:

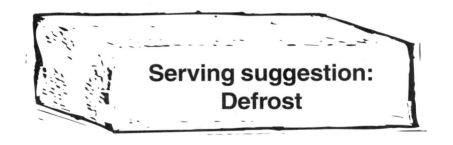

Serving suggestion: Defrost

Of course, it's only a suggestion ...

On a package of Christmas lights:

For indoor or outdoor use only

On a Swedish chainsaw:

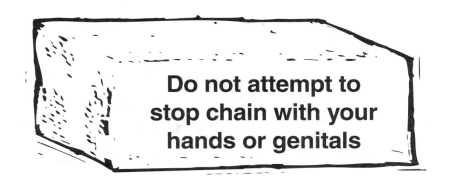

**Do not attempt to
stop chain with your
hands or genitals**

Stupid Classified Ads

OK, some of these are obviously typos, so we can't blame the advertisers.

But others are funny even with all the words spelled correctly.

Illiterate?
Write today for free help.

Our experienced Mom will care for your child. Fenced yard, meals and smacks included.

Stock up and save. Limit one.

**For sale: antique desk
suitable for lady with thick legs
and large drawers.**

Dog for sale: eats anything and is fond of children.

**Tired of cleaning yourself?
Let me do it.**

Used Cars:
Why go elsewhere to be
cheated? Come here first.

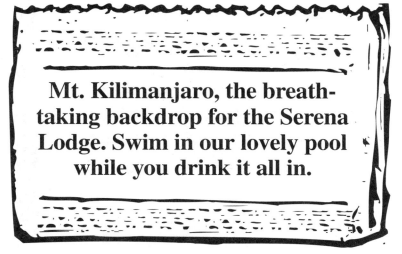

Mt. Kilimanjaro, the breath-taking backdrop for the Serena Lodge. Swim in our lovely pool while you drink it all in.

**Our bikinis are exciting,
They are simply the tops.**

**Man wanted to work
in dynamite factory.
Must be willing to travel.**

**Three-year-old teacher
needed for preschool.
Experience preferred.**

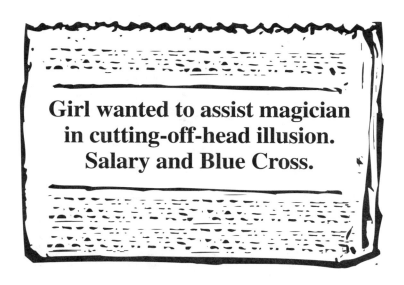

Girl wanted to assist magician in cutting-off-head illusion. Salary and Blue Cross.

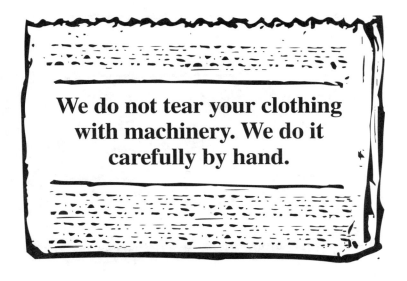

We do not tear your clothing with machinery. We do it carefully by hand.

**For Rent: Six room
hated apartment.**

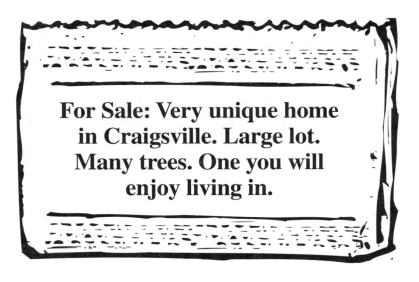

For Sale: Very unique home in Craigsville. Large lot. Many trees. One you will enjoy living in.

We will oil your sewing
machine and adjust tension
in your home for $1.00.

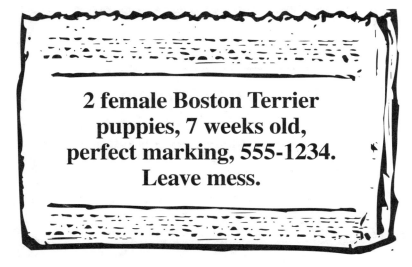

**2 female Boston Terrier
puppies, 7 weeks old,
perfect marking, 555-1234.
Leave mess.**

Lost: small apricot poodle.
Reward. Neutered.
Like one of the family.

A superb and inexpensive restaurant. Fine food expertly served by waitresses in appetizing forms.

Four-poster bed. 101 years old. Perfect for antique lover.

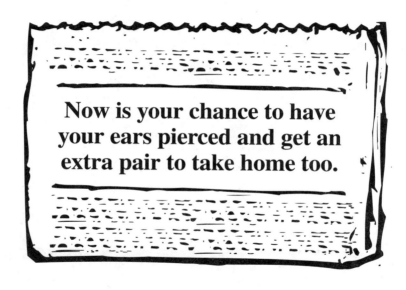

Now is your chance to have your ears pierced and get an extra pair to take home too.

Great Dames for sale.

**Have several very old
dresses from grandmother
in beautiful condition.**

147

**Wanted: hair cutter.
Excellent growth potential.**

148

**Wanted: Man to
take care of cow that
does not smoke or drink.**

Mixing bowl set designed to please a cook with round bottom for efficient beating.

**Semi-annual
after-Christmas sale.**

How to talk to your kids about sex, even if you've never done it before.

About Todd Hunt

Consider a man who started a financial services company in Chicago, grew it to 400 employees in three years, then sold it and opened a bookstore in Vermont ... after appearing on NBC's "Seinfeld" for three seasons.

Todd Hunt did not do any of those things.

But he *worked* for a financial services company in Chicago, *shopped* at a bookstore in Vermont ... and *watched* "Seinfeld" on NBC.

As an executive at Ogilvy & Mather, one of the world's largest advertising agencies, Todd learned the inner workings of communication.

Additional positions with an insurance

administrator, direct marketing company and ad department of a major retailer confirmed what he had suspected all along—people mess up communicating every day!

For 10 years, Todd ran his own marketing company in Chicago, selling insurance, credit accounts, conventions, seminars, theater tickets, memberships and other products and services to consumer and business audiences.

One day he discovered that people would pay him to tell funny, true stories about sales, customer service, leadership and change, that he garnered during his years in business. So now he does—speaking to hundreds of groups each year on how to communicate better with customers and employees to become more successful and make more money.

Now who doesn't want to hear that!